Alonzo Hall Quint

Three Sermons Preached in the North Congregational

Church

Alonzo Hall Quint

Three Sermons Preached in the North Congregational Church

ISBN/EAN: 9783744753951

Printed in Europe, USA, Canada, Australia, Japan

Cover: Foto ©Lupo / pixelio.de

More available books at **www.hansebooks.com**

NATIONAL SIN MUST BE EXPIATED BY NATIONAL CALAMITY.

WHAT PRESIDENT LINCOLN DID FOR HIS COUNTRY.

SOUTHERN CHIVALRY, AND WHAT THE NATION OUGHT TO DO WITH IT.

THREE SERMONS

PREACHED IN THE

NORTH CONGREGATIONAL CHURCH,

NEW BEDFORD, MASS.,

FAST DAY, APRIL 13, AND SUNDAY, APRIL 16, 1865.

BY ALONZO H. QUINT,

PASTOR.

NEW BEDFORD:

MERCURY JOB PRESS, 92 UNION STREET.

1865.

NATIONAL SIN MUST BE EXPIATED BY NATIONAL CALAMITY.

WHAT PRESIDENT LINCOLN DID FOR HIS COUNTRY.

SOUTHERN CHIVALRY, AND WHAT THE NATION OUGHT TO DO WITH IT.

THREE SERMONS

PREACHED IN THE

NORTH CONGREGATIONAL CHURCH,

NEW BEDFORD, MASS.,

FAST DAY, APRIL 13, AND SUNDAY, APRIL 16, 1865.

BY ALONZO H. QUINT,

PASTOR.

NEW BEDFORD:

MERCURY JOB PRESS, 92 UNION STREET.

1865.

NEW BEDFORD, April 14, 1865.

REV. A. H. QUINT:

DEAR SIR,—Having listened with much pleasure and profit to your discourse on the occasion of our annual State Fast, and believing the sentiments and principles so explicitly enunciated and enforced, will in their dissemination at this juncture in our National life, be productive of much good,—in accordance with numerously expressed wishes to that end, we respectfully request of you a copy for publication,

And are very truly yours,

JONA. BOURNE, JR.,	ANDREW MACKIE,
WARREN LADD,	A. H. SEABURY,
MOSES G. THOMAS,	OLIVER CROCKER,
JOS. R. READ,	WM. P. S. CADWELL,
I. D. HALL,	JOS. ARTHUR BEAUVAIS,
EDMUND RODMAN,	CORNELIUS DAVENPORT,
EDWARD HASKELL,	C. B. H. FESSENDEN,
JOHN HASTINGS,	FRED'K HOMER.

————

A subsequent request, April 17, included the two sermons preached on the Sabbath following the assassination of President Lincoln.

—

Messrs. JONATHAN BOURNE, Jr., and others:

DEAR SIRS,—I have always refused to give any sermons of mine to the press, except once, viz., when Sumpter fell. In that case I felt that the crisis should overrule personal reluctance.

So, present circumstances overcome my hesitation. Trusting to your kind assurances that they may do good, I place a copy at your disposal, with no time to remove the defects, of which no one will be more conscious than myself. Let them do their work, and then be forgotten.

Very respectfully yours,

ALONZO H. QUINT.

NEW BEDFORD, MASS., April 18, 1865.

I.

*NATIONAL SIN MUST BE EXPIATED BY NATIONAL CALAMITY.

Speak ye comfortably to Jerusalem, and cry unto her,
That her warfare is accomplished,
That her iniquity is pardoned,
For she hath received of the Lord's hand,
Double for all her sins.—ISAIAH XI: 2.

When a deputation not long since waited upon the head
of the nation, to present to him the assurance of the sympathy
and prayers of those whom they represented, they closed with
an expression of hope that the Lord would be on his side
and the nations'. "I have not," said the President in his
reply, "I have not given myself any care whether the Lord
is on our side; but I do feel anxious that myself and the
people should be upon the Lord's side."

Happy is that nation whose chief ruler is imbued with
such a principle; one able to perceive the distinction between
our asking God to be with us, and our determining to be
with God; between wishing God to favor a cause devised by
our own wishes, and making our cause to coincide with
God's wishes; between a statesmanship which has its origin
in human speculations and human selfishness, and one which
takes as a starting point the unerring principles of right and
justice.

The two kinds of statesmanship are totally different. Their
results are equally different. The one, starting in right, is
successful. "Happy is that people whose God is the Lord."
The other, starting in selfishness, ends in calamity.

---

* Preached on Fast Day, April 14, 1865.

I had intended, notwithstanding the character of this day as a day of penitence, to congratulate you upon the recent glorious victories of our arms. I had proposed to compare the present and the past. But yesterday's intimation of the President, that he will soon issue his call for a day of national thanksgiving, causes me to defer such an expression. Wait for that thanksgiving a little longer: you have patiently waited four weary years already, and now, every week is a week of new triumphs. Our warfare is well nigh accomplished; our iniquity is well nigh expiated. The double punishment for our sins, is almost closed. Then will I speak comfortably to Jerusalem. But before that day comes, let us look once more at our eventful illustrations of the truth that *national sin must have its expiation in national suffering*.

Well nigh accomplished. The sin *is* nearly "expiated and forgiven,"—for that is the real meaning of the words. Soon, now. The roar of cannon, and the rattle of musketry are soon to cease. The sabre and the bayonet shall flash no more. The charge of the rider shall end. The bivouac, the camp, the march, are soon to be a dream. The battalions shall hear no more the hoarse "forward." The shattered and glorious banners which we loved, shall droop in legislative halls. The mementoes of many a Manassas and Gettysburgh, shall be idle but eloquent toys. The grass shall grow green over the soldier's grave, and the bitter weeping shall mellow into loving sadness. Old comrades shall talk, by their firesides, of campaigns gone by, and sons shall love to hear their fathers tell, of a winter evening, when the snow is falling, and the wind is howling, of shelterless exposure to like storms and of exposure to the rattling storm of death.

That is, if the nation *remembers*. If justice shall prevail, and right be the rule, and God be acknowleged. For what formed the battalions, and beggared the arsenals, and blazoned the banners, and dug the graves? A nation's sin. Right had been forgotten. Integrity had poisoned the state. It was a righteous retribution. The iniquity had to be expiated.

I know that this is often ignored. Few governments practice upon it. England acts upon the reverse theory. It is the incarnation of selfishness: whose God is its belly, whose glory is in its shame. It has no principle. Tyrannical over the weak, fawning upon the strong; a hypocrite in morals; the very Pecksniff of nations.* Yet if it be said, England prospers—No. The day of reckoning is coming. Its knees already tremble, and its heart quakes. England is rotten with beggary. God's work may be slow, but it is sure. It was, in France. Generations rolled by, while the oppressor laughed at the oppressed, who cried " how long, O Lord, how long." But the day came, and revolutions ended in tyranny, and the tyranny rests on bayonets.

It was in the Convention which framed the Constitution of the United States, that the representatives of South Carolina, the now frightened and helpless remnant of the once haughty incarnation of tyranny, said—" Interest alone is the governing principle of nations. Religion and humanity have nothing to do with the question"—that is, of slavery.

But it was in that Convention, that Mason the grandfather of the now humbled and homeless rebel, said " As nations cannot be punished in the next world, they must in this. By an inevitable chain of causes and effects, Providence punishes national sins by national calamities."

The latter is true. It is impossible for a nation which acts unjustly, to be permanently strong. Its life is in righteousness. To sin is to sap the strength of national existence. Especially is this so in a government of the people. Public virtue is then the soul of public power. As the people are, so will be the rulers. And as the spirit of the nation is, so will be its vigor; its influence at home, and its respect abroad. This is a general fact. The decay of principle in the national life is the decay of might.

Never were the two more distinctly set forth than in the words I have quoted from the representatives of Virginia and South Carolina. Happy had it been if the Virginia of that

---

*If anybody else has been suprised at the course of England, in the time of our national troubles, I am sure I have not. I believe now, as I did twenty years ago, and no more strongly now than then, that the continued prosperity of England, as then and now governed, would be a curse to the world.

day had prevailed. For the Virginia then, was the home of that Washington who left his slaves free; of that Jefferson who trembled for his country when he thought that God was just. While the South Carolina of that day is the South Carolina of later days, soulless, reckless, alike devoid of honor and of truth.

But South Carolina then prevailed. And it is easy to see, not only the general principle that justice is essential to public power, but how the very sins committed, come themselves to be the instruments of punishment.

I. Our fault was, in the very formation of the government, in not placing it on the platform of justice; and that mistake was the instrument of its own penalty.

The majority in that convention were opposed to slavery. Some of these had just been fighting for liberty. Yet considerations of mere expediency prevailed. South Carolina and Georgia demanded the right to send ship to Africa, steal its unoffending inhabitants, bring them to America, and consign them and their descendants to perpetual slavery. They said in explicit language, " No slave trade, no Union." So for union, the slave trade was allowed for a generation. South Carolina and Georgia demanded a clause for the return of fugitives. " No return of fugitives, no Union." So the constitution was cursed with that which made us the betrayers of a helpless fugitive. They demanded extra political power in a proportion to their number of slaves. " No such allowance, no Union." So they get their demands.

Some say that they gave us a kind of equivalent; we then had a price of blood. It was to favor the shipping interest of the North. *That* quieted the conscience. That, and to make a union between light and darkness, a covenant with hell.

Men might have seen that such a union had in it a curse. They might have known that a government which violated the cardinal principles of right could not prosper in the end. Well was it said by an eminent statesman,—" when we are founding States, all these laws must be brought to the standard of the laws of God, must be tried by that standard, and must stand or fall by it." But they forgot that. They forgot that " He that stealeth a man, and selleth him, he shall surely be put to death." They forgot that the "law was made for man-stealers." They forgot that "thou shalt not return unto his master the servant who is escaped from his master; he shall dwell with thee, thou shalt not oppress him." They forgot that "God hath made of one blood all the nations of the earth." They gathered together all the noble things they had ever done for liberty, and trod them under their feet. To gain South Carolina and Georgia, they forgot the laws of God.

How well did it work? When this time of trial came, South Carolina was the first to secede, and Georgia the second. South Carolina opened the war, and Georgia was the first to send re-inforcements in the carnival of treason. We gained South Carolina in that first lapse from right: she gave us four years of such war as the world never saw. How do you like it? We gained a shipping interest. It was a gain. But in that very thing of temptation came the penalty. You men of New Bedford, what think you of your burning vessels, of your scattered commerce? The very wealth the fathers sold righteousness for, has lit up the ocean with its fires.

In that departure, we yielded to slavery. In God's righteous judgment, he has made that slavery the very instrument of our punishment. *It* made this war. *It* fired the southern hearts. *It* crazed their minds. *It* added to southern strength. *It* raised their crops to feed the southern armies. *It* doubled their forces. When we waited weeks in front of Yorktown, *it* had built their works. When we were hurled back from the ravine of death, at Fredericksburg, *it* had crowned the heights with lines of defence. When we lost our thousands at Donelson, *it* had, as their General said, done the labor, so that he could drill his raw men for the work of slaughter. I saw the works at Winchester, which enabled Johnston to join Beauregard and win the battle of Bull Run; slaves built them. I saw the lines at Fredericksburg, which slaves had built. I saw the forts, redoubts, rifle-pits, and breastworks at Resacca, which slaves had built. The slavery we had allowed, slaughtered our young men and filled our land with widows and orphans. In all of it, God said, the sin you agreed to shall be your curse. What were South Carolina and Georgia to the everlasting law of God? You gained two states but you gained a curse.

II. The corruption which followed and which was admitted into government itself, has worked its legitimate result.

The two principles had come in conflict in the beginning. Right had been yielded. Expediency had conquered. That miserable expediency which is the unfailing refuge, when a mean or a cowardly thing is to be done. There is a place for expediency; but it is when two things are equally morally right; not when one is right and the other is wrong. Admit the wrong, because it seems expedient, and you have weakened your manliness; you have vitiated your life. When the nation in its very organic paper, acted on expediency—apparent self-interest, that is,—it *made* that the standard of public virtue. It simply said,—our rule is, do what self desires. What apt scholars it found, what multitudes willing to apply that to the individual, it is needless to say. What corruption in politics, it made. How uselessly the fathers tried to stay the tide of wrong. All this it is needless to review.

In the various compromises was corruption. Moral principle was ignored. Doubtless many believed, sincerely, that they were doing a moral duty. But multitudes knew that at the best it was a violation of right, to preserve the trembling union; and at the *most*, it was the trading of politicians in office and profit; a bid for the presidency here and a bid for party power there; for offices in Washington, and customs in New Bedford. The words of true men, were disregarded. The warnings of the past were unheeded. They triumphed in oppression : they became vain in robbery.

The nation found its legitimate penalty. I have heard of an inhuman father, who with his family was pursued by rave-neous wolves. How the sledge was urged faster and faster, but the wolves gained. How, to save a part alive, he threw one child to the wolves. They snapped at it; they stopped; they devoured it. On again, after this momentary pause; another child; and the same momentary relief. And yet a third; and alas, a fourth. And at last, the man and his wife; only the driver escaped to tell the tale. So did the nation. It remorselessly consigned tract after tract, to the dominion of the slave holding wolves; millions at once to the lash and chain. But every gift merely whetted the appetite of the devourers, and at last, they laid their teeth on the nation itself. Then, in God's mercy, it awoke and it found strength: but not, until by the resurrection of liberty, it called back to life the children it had foully abandoned; and not until the penalty of its successive crimes was mercilessly exacted. The very sin which the nation thought had secured peace in 1789, demanded a new victim in 1820; and that, in 1845, and that, in 1850, and that found its crowning infamy in 1857, when the Supreme Court bowed at last. One yielding of principle had demanded another, and the sin was its own punishment.

This corruption was seen in choice of public servants. It became rare, and still rarer to find men called into public life because the country needed them. Most of them needed the country, and its purse. How seldom was one spontaneously called for? so seldom that it was a marked case where a man of stainless private life, of public virtue, above suspicion, of sound mind, was selected by the people to represent them in Congress. And that such a man has preserved this honor in the atmosphere of Washington, you wondered. You remember to what our Congress had degenerated. You remember its drunkenness, its pistols, its knives, its bargains, and its prizes; its trucklings and its snap of the whip. Until "northern dough-faces" was the most suitable epithet which could be found.

And in allowing this corruption, the nation finds its punishment. A few bonded slave drivers ruled. They dictated laws. They made war and peace. They occupied the best chairs. The controlled the foreign policy. And the great parties, when a man's conscience stood up for what he thought right as to liberty, threw him off, lest the southern section of the party should abandon *them*. Right ceased to rule. Wrong was triumphant. The free spirit fretted and chafed, but is was helpless. It had taken the "old man of the sea" upon its back, just to cross the stream; and it found a permanent master who choked his victim when he hesitated to obey.

This spirit reached its climax at last. Not when the course of things silently yielded to such wrong. Not when bad men got offices. Not even when the impious maxim "our country, right or wrong" was the delirious shout of many a crazy thousand. But it did, when politicians scoffed at truth, and cried "there is no higher law than that of the country;" and partisans echoed "no higher law;" and the pulpits blasphemely repeated "no higher law." Many men in all parties shuddered. I thank God, that however I had chosen betwen the two great parties in the country, I said, "*this* is blasphemy. There *is* a higher law. When conscience is sure it cannot obey the laws, let it silently suffer its penalty, but let it not disobey God." When Tract Societies came to be hopelessly corrupt, and Boards of Missions had communicants in their churches, who burnt slaves at the stake; when ministers outraged conscience and truth by apologizing for slavery; when churches were worshipping in the house of Baal; then there brooded over our country clouds of divine wrath. The air grew heavy. It seemed hard to breathe. The blackness grew fearfully. Then the heavy roll of the thunder crashed. Then the forked lightning played. Tempests howled, and fire struck, and the track ofthe fierce storm ploughed furrows of wrath.

But not until God made our own folly the instrument of our punishment. Corruption had placed in offices of trust and power, men unfit to exercise government. We found the result. When the crazy spirit of rebellion, which the nation had itself fostered by compromises, took form, then it found convenient to it the powers that were. It wanted arms, and treason in the war office sent them to rebel arsenals; it wanted the navy scattered, and it had been scattered to the

ends of the earth. It wanted the army helpless, and treason
sent it away. It wanted no acts taken to support the laws,
and imbecility sat in the chair of the executive. It wanted
helpers, and the public offices were full of traitors. It wanted
northern sympathies, and northern demagogues said that the
streets north would run with blood before a man should leave
them to coerce the rebels. It wanted men to weaken the
power of the government, and some northern men for four
years have either kept silent when their country was in the
time of its sore calamity, when every loyal man, either by
his voice, his money, or his right arm, came to his country's
help; or, not silent were northern men, assaulting the government with abuse, discouraging the efforts of the loyal, active-
ly sympathizing with rebellion, and so covertly slaughtering
their brothers in the field. The race called " copperheads,"
traitorous enough to ruin their country, but too cowardly to
take arms like men and stand with Lee—they were the evidence of the degradation to which public morality had come
when it could produce so vile, so mean, so abject, so cowardly
a being as a "copperhead." Yet they were the inevitable result of the national compromises. There are few now. They
have always been loyal. They wonder that any one thought
they were not. But the memory of an outraged people will
not soon forget how, in the terribly gloomy days, in the midst
of the war, these men did what they dared to do, to weaken
the hands of the country. If I speak strongly on this, remember that I have seen my comrades in death before a foe
whom these men were stengthening; remember that I have
laid those noble men under the sod, and knew when I did it,
that northern sympathy had nerved the arms that shot the
bullets. The punishment was inevitable. The wrongs of
millions cried to heaven for redress. The consenting to evil
had poisoned the state.

But God had purposes of mercy. Those purposes were
worked out, not in saying " you are forgiven," for that would
not remove the evil; not in the gentle gray and then the
twilight, and then ruddy and golden streaks of the rising sun,
and then calm day; not in gentle dews and showers; but

night came, heavy, hard, and bleak; tempest came, sharp, severe, fiery; earthquake and volcano came; the skies were lighted, but it was with the lurid flame of wrath; the earth was watered, but it was with deluge.

So God brought us to see the sin.

And in the progress of this war, we see also the gradual return to right. The sin is expiated. But until expiated and abandoned, it could not be forgiven. The main features as to success, I think, show plainly God's providence.

We began with a hearty, noble outburst of loyalty. It was a kind of blind instinct of love for our flag, that God made use of, to keep the heart of the nation steady, and to nerve us in many a trying time. The sovereignty of the nation was in the flag and that sovereignty we said, shall be preserved. So it went on, but we never met with settled progress until that banner became identified with liberty.

We cannot connect events too closely. Omniscience only can do that. We can see only the broad current. But we can see some strange coincidences. The week of that disastrous battle of Bull Run, it was sad, but I saw fugitive slaves returned to their rebel masters that week. The general, who took command of our armies then, had proclaimed that he would suppress slave revolts "with an iron hand;" it was the policy of the government, but he, its instrument, was baffled in every attempt to touch the rebel power. His highest day was when he hurled back the fiery invasion at Antietam. In the west no important success was had until a General was sent to New Orleans, who believed in the rights of man. That terribly slaughtering day at Shiloh you remember; and its subsequent blundering campaign, which happened, says a witness " from the exclusion of contrabands." Almost all we did for nearly two years was to hold our own. God did not permit any invasion of us to succeed, but that was all.

But from the time the proclamation of emancipation was issued, the current of affairs changed. We soon made substantial progress when those who believed in justice took command. It requires no need of a special interposition of divine Providence to see what causes and effects could do.

When generals took advantage of their own faith, they crippled the enemy in his strongest yet weakest points. The government had the sympathies of millions of people in the enemy's own land. This was the natural sequence. So, too, is the fact, as one who knew every item of foreign affairs told me, that the emancipation proclamation was all that prevented recognition of the slave empire by great foreign powers; they dared not then go against the moral sense of the world. But while we can see natural causes at work, it is not presumptuous to believe that God looked with favor on a nation that had taken the position of justice, He who had said "let my people go." The prayers and tears of millions went up to Him. He said to us,—pause until you do justice; you shall be baffled until you do justice; you shall strive but you shall not advance. "Let my people go." I tell you I would rather have the prayers of those bondmen to the Lord of Hosts, on our side, than to have a hundred thousand more veterans. Eternity alone can tell what a power at the throne of God were the prayers of the bondman. Only as we recognised his claim to manhood, did we advance.

But then when we said " You are free;" when we placed the musket in his hands, and made him that high type of a man — a soldier, we moved forward. The pillar of cloud by day and the pillar of fire by night were with us. The flag we bore was the symbol of freedom, and we had God's benediction. Then it opened the Mississippi river on the birthday of the nation; then that birthday witnessed Lee's rapid flight from Gettysburg; when Meade followed him back as he recrossed the river for the last time, it was with the flag of freedom; when Hooker's starred division scaled Lookout, and fought above the mountain mists, it was under the flag of freedom; when Missionary ridge was swept by the advancing line, the old grave of a proslavery mission was won to freedom; Chattanooga's fastnesses were fortified impregnably for freedom; when Sherman assailed Rocky face it was for freedom; when he won the hard lines of Resacca it was with freedom; Dallas and Kenesaw gave way to the advancing hosts of freedom; Atlanta fell for freedom; the adventurous march through Georgia—it was the signal of freedom to scores of thousands, and the auction block of Savannah is a trophy of freedom, before which, in years to come, men will wonder that a christian nation ever allowed such infamy; when Grant made Virginia a desolation, and sat down at Petersburg; when he swept through their works and into Richmond; when the flower of the rebel power surrendered; and when the rebel tyrant became a fugitive and a wanderer, the nations of the earth know that it was not until the national Congress had declared that "slavery" was dead.

But to reach this point there was double punishment for all our sins. If expiation can ever move the pity of God, truly we have gained it. Suffering and calamity; burden of debt equal to the named value of every slave; expenditure equalling every dollar ever won out of the sweat of the oppressed; blood in torrents, to which the blood of the lash had the provocative; graves; widows, orphans, weeping men and women of gray hairs. Thank God that the iniquity is expiated; that the sin is forgiven; that the sun shines again, for it had to be borne.

To-day is the first fast day such as God's has chosen. For many a year He said "Is not this the fast that I have chosen, to loose the bands of wickedness; to undo the heavy burdens; and to let the oppressed go free; and that ye break every yoke?" But for many a year we refused to hearken; we were proud and haughty. But since this last annual occasion, the deed of Congress has said "Lord, we *do* loose the bands of wickedness; we *do* undo the heavy burdens; we *do* let the oppressed go free; we *do* break every yoke." This is the fast that God has chosen. We are on the Lord's side at last. We can humble ourselves for past wrong properly and in a right spirit, It was never enough to confess our sins; "Whoso confesseth and *forsaketh* them shall have mercy." God brought us to forsake them. Partly it was because he showed us that success would be impossible, and useless if possible, so long as we left unharmed the great power which exalted itself against God; but with many it was the conviction that this sin stood in the way, and even those who felt bound by constitutional obligation, rejoiced that that yoke the oppressor had himself broken.

Yet is there no more to do? God has taught us that national sin must be expiated. If we do not forsake all wrong the sin remaining will work penalty. There is yet something to do; there are men who still persist in maintaining slavery, so far as to vote in Legislatures against a constitutional way of removing it. Let all such and all who sympathise with them, repent. If there is one who justifies slavery, if one who does not see that slavery is a sin, not merely a calamity, let him repent in sorrow and humility; let him say, Oh Thou "who came to preach deliverance to the captive," have mercy on me, for I have forgotten my Master's spirit. — But the question is now to be met, how to preserve what we have gained, and how shall we reconstruct? I am sorry to see any indications of a sentiment that would re-form the South, without securing justice. We cannot ignore the manhood of the former slave. He is a man; he must be treated as a man; there is no reason why he should not. The blacks of the South are the equals in intelligence and ability, and the superiors in uprightness and religion, of the whites of the South.* Every word that mentions color should be erased from the Statute books. In re-forming State government, no distinction of race ought to be allowed for a moment. Manhood, not color, is the only just foundation for government. When re-made states come with organic laws not providing for equality in civil rights, the nation should say " No, you shall not despise any man ; you do sin against that God who made of one blood all the nations of the earth ; you do violate that declaration also which says 'That all men are created free and equal ;' you shall stand on simple justice, or you shall never enter the Congress of the United States." This should the people demand; this, they should make every offi-

---

* In the course of observations, while in the service, I soon became satisfied of this truth. After leaving out the exceptional cases of high culture (which the blacks are not allowed,) I am sure that the average intellect and thrift of the blacks is superior to that of the whites. As to honor, there is no comparison. Slavery has done the character of the whites far more harm than it has that of the blacks.

cial hear; this, they should stand fast to, unless they wish more of the wrath of God. It is no matter, as to the foundation of morals, what state government is respected, this or that; but it is vital, that the claim of every man to manhood shall be recognised. If not, " Then we looked for peace, but no good came; and for a time of health, and behold trouble."

For God would work. National sin would work national calamity. If you neglect our friends, who have guided our escaped prisoners from their bondage, who have fed our hungry soldiers and given them water to drink, who have told our generals of the enemy at the risk of life, where is justice? If you disfranchise the only really loyal portion of the South, if you leave all power in the hands of the repentant rebels, half perjured, and half merely subjugated, where is safety? How before they control every State government at the South? How long before they are strong enough to bargain with Northern demagogues? How long before you are hampered with a keen, persistent, traitorous foe in your Capitol? It needs no prophetic power to see this sure result.

This dire calamity is not yet ended, unless we have learned that the foundation of this struggle was deeper than Acts, or Constitution, or even slavery itself, — the question of Equal Rights. The lesson of this suffering is not learned, unless we have determined to recognise the simple rights of Manhood. Slavery is but an incident; respect for Manhood is a principle.

If we think we are more richly endowed than some others, yet, as we treat the meanest of God's creatures, so will He treat us. For, " Inasmuch as ye have done it unto one of the least of these My brethren, ye have done it unto Me."

II

*What President Lincoln Did for his Country.

Thou shalt view the land before thee; but thou shalt not go thither unto the land. — Deuteronomy, xxxii: 52.

Our bells rang merrily that morning. They waked us, in the gray dawn, with their laughing peals. Our flags, in multitudes, gaily flew out in the breeze. The guns thundered the joyful news. Our children shouted in patriotic glee, and the old men were children. The rains came that day, but it was sunshine.

But, yesterday morn, in the gray dawn, the saddened bells tolled heavily. The flags hung listlessly, in black. The guns wait, in grim sorrow, to boom their funeral echo. The very children were subdued to quiet, and the old men wept. The sun shone, but it was darkness.

For, a just, a good, and a great man, had passed away. The head of the nation, too. The nation's honest, unselfish, true, leader had gone; with his large, warm heart; his womanly tenderness; his quiet patience; his long foresight. Gone in a way which shocked the nation's heart.

But turn, for a little time, to the words of the text. They were said to Moses. The Moses who had been chosen of God to be, after gradual preparation, the leader of Israel; who had been slow of heart, and diffident of spirit, to undertake the momentous work, in view of those severe trials which he saw nigh at hand; the Moses who had led the people out of the land of Egypt, and through the Red Sea; the Moses who,

---

*Preached Sunday morning, April 16, 1865.

2

in years of wandering and in oft troubles, had been a wise and discreet ruler; the Moses who had succeeded in suppressing riotous and factious opposition to proper authority; the Moses whose faith was tried, and stood, in dark days; the Moses who had found bread in the desert, and at whose smiting, the waters gushed from the rock; the Moses chosen of God to declare His law, and who had talked with God. He, when the wanderings were well nigh over, and the promised land near, by command of God ascended Mount Nebo, to the top of Pisgah, and to him the Lord showed the land, and said, " This is the land — I have caused thee to see it with thine eyes, but thou shalt not go over thither." So there the servant of the Lord died, and the children of Israel wept for Moses.

Our leader saw the promised land, but was never to enter it. The sea, desert, the strifes and seditions, were past; and the land of plenty was before the people. But on Pisgah he died.

I am not careful to press the points of resemblance; much less to compare the guidance of God in our case, with the inspiration of the prophet. But these points of resemblance touch involuntarily. In the evident hand of God in the choice of leader; in the diffidence and meekness; in the kindness of heart; in the foresight and judgment; in the trials and obstacles; in the revelation of holy principles; in the final success; and in the untimely fate, — as to personal qualities and peculiar experience, no other person in our history, to say the least, has so nearly resembled the great Hebrew, as our own wise, unpretending, devout, President.

Because thus cut off was his life unfinished? Who shall say that of Moses. With us as with the Hebrew, our leader's life was a completed epic. The result was not to be enjoyed by him, but his work was done.

Of the cruel, devilish way in which the President was murdered, I do not propose to speak now. I must separate the themes, if I would not be unfitted by righteous wrath to say what I wish this morning. Forget it, for this hour; and if afternoon comes, I hope to then describe the people who have done this thing, and tell what I conceive to be the duty of the nation as to them. Now let us try to see how posterity will contrast the day Abraham Lincoln took the charge of the government with that on which he left it.

I. Abraham Lincoln found this government well nigh ruined ; against tremendous obstacles, he left it powerful.

Have you forgotten those dark days of 1860-1 ? How treason was boasting itself? How State after State seceded? How their vaunts ridiculed northern valor ? How the bewildered nation gazed at itself benumbed? How the south and hell held jubilee, and the oppressed and heaven mourned ? How we asked ourselves painfully, what do our authorities mean? How imbecility sat in the Executive chair, and the " Pennsylvania snake " (as Andrew Jackson called him) declared that the government had no right to coerce rebels ? How the London paper rejoiced, " the American bubble has burst ? " How foreign powers believed that the great republic was dead ? I have not forgotten it. I slept better afterwards, on the ground, and under the sound of artillery, than I did those wearisome nights.

To such a government did Abraham Lincoln go. When he paused on the road now and then, as crowds demanded to see him, it was to ask their prayers for him, in view of the black clouds he saw were soon to burst. He escaped assassination only by eluding the conspirators. And he took the oath of office, guarded by such troops as the old Lieutenant General could hastily collect.

He found his capital city mainly rebel in sentiment. He found a third of his country in rebellion. He found no army ; the brave little one that had been, had been scattered, to fall, most of it, a helpless prey. He found few ships, and some of those under rebel guns; the navy had been scattered too. He found few arms; a rebel Secretary had moved them south. He found poor credit; it had fallen with the honor of the government. He found traitors in every department; every office full of rebels. He found doubt and distrust everywhere ; everywhere gloom and fear.

Before he was well seated in the chair of government, ten States were in rebellion. All the southern forts, save two, were in the hands of the enemy. The mints, the arsenals, the treasuries, southward, were gone. The way from the north to the Capital was broken. The troops he called for, were refused by some States, and those that first came were attacked in the chief city of a State, which full of treachery, had not seceded. A new government was inaugurated with all pomp, and the Potomac and the Ohio were the virtual boundaries of the republic. When one regiment, reaching Washington by a circuitous course, entered into the doors of the vast capitol, "it seemed," said an eye witness, "as though they were gone into a tomb."

But his heart was not dismayed. They laughed at his first call for soldiers. It was not the call we wanted. But he knew that a million more were ready, and he was not fearful. He was God's chosen instrument. Selected over so many public men to whom the nation had looked,— it seems to have been because we needed a patient, honest, undisturbed man. He set himself to his duty. Not a great man, to look at. An unpretending one; somewhat awkward; without the magnetic charm of a personal electricity; but a true, faithful, courageous man, whose hand, when you took it, you felt to be the hand of an honest man. He had not the scholarly culture of a Davis, but he never perjured himself; nor the refinement of a Lee, but he never turned traitor; not the eloquence of a Stephens, but he never lied.

Over the river was a beautiful mansion, which was Lee's home, when he deserted his post. From Arlington Heights, a rifled piece would throw a shot to the President's house; and Arlington Heights were in rebel power. Five miles below, on the Potomac, was Alexandria; you can see it down the river,— and there was the rebel flag. A day's march off was Fairfax, and there the rebel forces were gathering. Down the river to Occoquan, rebel batteries soon closed the avenues to the sea. Up the river, were the arsenals of Harper's Ferry; and rebels held them. In the west, you could not go far below St. Louis on the father of waters, and Kentucky was trodden by rebel armies.

Almost beseiged in his capital. But the true man never quailed. He relied on the people, and on God. He gathered troops. He multiplied armories. He bought and built vessels.

Baffled., Back pour in dismay a routed army from Bull Run; a torrent without shape; over the Long Bridge, and into Washington; an exultant and triumphant foe at their heels. In Missouri, forts fall. And between the two points, there is no attempt to advance. The campaign is a failure, outwardly. But he never doubts. He gathers more men. He makes more guns. He builds more ships. He selects new generals.

There were gloomy times afterwards. I remember when, near Alexandria, with Lee's victorious legions pressing us back from the disastrous fields of Cedar Mountain and Manassas, and with us the returned army which had been baffled on the Peninsula, that a Senator of the United States said in our camp, "this war is now only a question of boun-daries." So it was with Abraham Lincoln. But his boun-daries included all he had sworn to preserve; the Canada line on the north, and the Gulf on the south; the Atlantic on the east, and the Pacific on the west. His simple minded patience swayed Senators. One general fails? He tries another. One naval leader fails? Another hoists the broad pennant. With him it was the question of a nation's life and death.

You who were at home, know little, but imagine much, of a soldier's hard fare, and shelterless nights, and daily dangers. I have seen something of them. They are severe. But, when I have seen the care marked face of the man, before whom generals doffed their hats, and the drums ruffled, and the battle-scarred banners bowed, I have thought I would rather bear the lot of the soldier, than to live with *him* in the nation's mansion house, and sit at his table, — to hear his soldiers' reveille every morning and tattoo every night, an-swered by the taunting drum-corps of rebel armies on a line of a thousand miles. None but a great man could have borne it.

He was perplexed by foreign relations. The great powers who had haughtily scoffed at America because of its slavery, their governments backed up by whining Christians — became slavery's allies. How swift they were to give belligerent rights to slaveholding rebels! How eager to pick flaws enough to give them — especially England — some face to interfere. Their builders built pirates. Their ports sheltered pirates. Their merchants sent goods. In every battle, we fought British guns, and British powder; and British clothing the traitors wore, and British shoes were on their feet; and British sympathy cheered their hearts. Their very money, British engravers engraved, and British printers printed. For all of which thanks be to God, the day of righteous retribution cometh. But the perplexities which our President found, were enormous. Fortunately he had called to his aid one whose prudence, candor, and sense, interpreted his own. Through these difficulties, the President steered. Safely he led us through. Sometimes we thought him too prudent; but we were mistaken. He was not timid; only cautious. When deference would have been unmanly, his minister at the Court of St. James had authority to say, "if these rams leave port, it is war!"

He had trials in the loyal states. Party feeling came to be high. The first gush of enthusiastic reverence for the flag shut down, for a time, the talk of traitors and cowards. But that passed off. The times which tried men's souls came. Then the faint hearted fell off. Then the old party leaders tried to resume power. They deceived some, under specious pretences. By and by, calumny, abuse, and insults, were thick as snow-flakes of a winter's day. But no word of anger escaped his breast at these! It was in sorrow that he said, Father forgive them; they know not what they do! They were savage, perhaps, most of all, when his darling child lay a-dying, and the father walked the floor in anguish hour after hour, with all these troubles upon him,—I knew of these things then, — and, under the crushing load he used to bow before God, and pray in agony. And then calmly turn away, and in war office or navy, consider everything his country's need demanded, as though no weight bore him down. He cast his burden on the Lord, and the Lord sustained him.

Even when the Empire State led the way, by its vote, in seeming disapproval, and it seemed to some as if the people were tired of the struggle, he believed that it was not so. He saw under the surface, and knew that even misled men would reconsider. Riots and burnings in his chief city,—a Governor who appropriately called the men burning asylums and killing orphans, "my friends,"—and I preached and prayed in City Hall Park while the sentries walked past and our arms were stacked in lines, and the guns were ready to wheel in an instant into the streets of the city,—all those riots and murders in opposition to filling our armies, did not move him from his course. When timid copperheads merely failed to sustain their country; and bolder copperheads gave all their cowardly hearts dare give, their words, against their country; when they complained of the arrests of northern traitors, though they knew that if justice were done, the whole viperous brood would hang higher than Haman,—the calm, well-poised mind of the chief held to its work, to save his country, their and your children. He knew whom he could trust; the army,—that glorious one whose patient endurance is crowned at Richmond; and that other which rolled the foe back through Kentucky, through Tennesee, over the hills of Chattanooga, through the heart of Georgia, and broke the empty shell; the soldiers, whose burning hearts, though sad with change of beloved leaders, often said,—lead us against the treacherous men at home; find us those who are helping traitors; and the bayon'et shall end their treason. He knew whom he could trust; the navy, such a gallant navy as the world never surpassed. He knew whom he could trust; the people,—in their imperial patriotism; even that part sometimes warped a little by ill-success, but sure to come right again; all the people, of every party, all except the Valladinghams, and the Touceys, whom this country will remember, and with them every man who failed that country in its time of wo. He knew whom he could trust; God! And to God he gave himself and his life.

We see the results. There were mistakes all along. Wrong men were sometimes selected. Unfortunate acts were sometimes done. Who can wonder? But we see the result. He left his country, for a better, that is, a heavenly. But he left it powerful. The voice of faction was heard only like the distant muttering of the ended storm; or like the scattering and sullen shots of a retreating foe when the battle is over. He left the nation strong in military array. Its invincible veterans, when he died, could have dared the world. Its generals are the masters of war. Its arsenals are full to bursting. Its navies frighten the former mistress of the seas. Its admirals are the heroes of the ocean, and its sailors range up to the forts and hurl their canister into the very embrasures. Its credit is practically unlimited. Its resources are like the bread in the desert and the water from the rock. Abroad, the nations are aghast at the resurrection of the great democracy. He could say, at last, as to harbors and vessels, "with what measure ye mete, it shall be measured to you again;" and the man who had never taken a backward step in all his career, would have made good his word. He left the American flag flying over every one of the old forts, and he had built a multitude of new ones. New Orleans, Savannah, Charleston, were ours. The capital of the Confederacy he had entered; the main army of the rebellion was captured, and the rebel President was a fugitive. On that very day in which he fell, the same old flag had been flung to the breeze on Sumpter which four years before had come down, and the same man who had lowered it, had raised it again.

Such things had he accomplished. Not he alone; the people did it. Wise public men did it. God did it. But he was the chosen of God and the people, to lead. That people trusted him. They put into his hands such unprecedented powers, in perfect confidence that not a single selfish, ambitious, or vindictive motive would ever sully his mind. No one even ventured to charge him with corruption. Not a particle of illegitimate influence did he attempt to wield. He was not a great leader, as such; not like Jackson, more like Washington; calm, self-poised, a medium between extremes, generous, conciliatory, slow sometimes, but faithful, persistent, and true; not a genius, but a truly great man. He was not a cipher in his cabinet, as some Presidents have been. He consulted them, but he decided for himself. His policy was *his*. These qualities God saw we needed; with them, he took the government almost ruined; he left it a great power.

II. Abraham Lincoln found this country a slave country; he left it free.

I reminded you, last Thursday, how this country had always been cursed with slavery. I told you then, of the haughty supremacy of the slave power. I never believed, nor do I now, that there was no slavery in the constitution. It seems to me to be there as clearly as legal terms could put it there, and proved by the debates of those who made that instrument. The Supreme Court has decided that question, too.

When Abraham Lincoln was chosen President, the people said, by that choice, that slavery should not be extended. The States which loved it might keep it. The obligations of the constitution we will keep sacred; the fugitive we will return to his master. This was the platform of the party which elected him. That party's sympathies were with freedom, but the platform was "conservative." I always doubted the legal rightness of even their own plank of freedom,—as to the territories; but the Supreme Court could have settled that, if a case should come to test any law made in its spirit.

True, the South was not satisfied. State after State seceded, on lying pretences,— the slave question being their pretext only. But their secession did not make the nation free; for the Constitution still claimed them, and they could have come back with new guarantees. Even if they had gone entirely, it would not have left us free. For Maryland and Delaware remained, and still claimed protection for slave property.

When the new President reached Washington, the flag which flew over the Capitol, had its twin flying over the slave pen. The flag! you see it now drooped in sorrow — before you. This centre of a soldier's and a patriot's love,—its copy used to mark the slave mart, as much as to say,—and it did say it truly,—the United States sanctions this trade in its very capital, and in its exclusive district, the nation makes special laws to protect it; a code one which, in its merciless provisions, as far as transcends ordinary slave legislation, as the Inquisition did the proceedings of a New England court. To Henry Wilson belongs the transcendent honor of exploring, exposing, and crushing it.

It would be wrong to suppose that the President when he went to Washington, had any intention of destroying slavery. His party, his platform, forbade it. He was a conservative man. He felt bound by law not to interfere. But his merit was, that he loved liberty himself. He believed in freedom. And it was his purpose to give the government, what it never had, a bias to liberty. He was mistaken in the great point. Most were mistaken. To give slavery free range within certain defined limits, is as wise as to give a prairie fire the right to burn within certain limits, and those limits bound by a board fence; as wise as to say to a pestilence in your city,—you shall have free range within certain boundaries, and those boundaries are marked by a chalk line on the pavement. That motto "Freedom national, Slavery sectional," was a great step; but it was wrong in principle. Slavery was either national or no-where. If it had a right to live in the States, it had a right, I think, to go into those territories which were surrendered by those whose local law allowed slavery. The true ground was that it had no claim anywhere; and that it was the duty of the government to secure the rights of every inhabitant on our soil. Slavery's legal claim was a defiance of Almighty God.

Abraham Lincoln learned well. His heart was always right. So, as fast as obstacles were removed, so fast did liberty advance. He watched the course of events, and went on step by step. He tried to have the slaves set free by purchase. Thank God, it was not done. Then, slaves made free by the progress of arms, should remain free. By and by, the emancipation proclamation covered all slaves in the rebellious states. And at last the great act of Congress did all it could do, to extirpate slavery from the whole land. If you think that he went too slow, — that it was not until September, 1862, that his great proclamation came, — remember that he had felt bound by law, and that only as the rebel line of conduct freed him from restraint, did he feel at liberty. His slowness was honest. Remember, too, how hard it is to educate a nation. It is not an easy thing for men to break their old political alliances, and throw to the winds their life-long dogmas. Many of you have done it; you deserve praise for it. But such a thing takes time, except when some Sumpterlike shock startles us out of consistency. Consistency? I don't want to be *consistent*; I want to be *right*. If my course has been mistaken, I am not ashamed to say so.

Some of the veterans of liberty think he was too slow. It is the day of your triumph; that you bear the triumph so meekly is to *your* credit. The President's course was a medium one. I think he was too cautious. And this illustrates one want in him, I suppose. He did not strike out boldly, when the people wanted to be led. The atoms were in confusion, waiting for him to crystallize them. A Jackson would have placed himself at the head of the legions, and said, "this I mean to do; follow me!" And the people would have followed. Lacking this element, he did not excite enthusiasm; though he secured respect. He was not a brilliant, but a safe leader. But he was like Jackson in this,—that when he had decided, no power could move him a hair's breadth. The storms of faction raged around him, and dashed all over him; but when the waves fell, he was still steady and calm as the rock.

He did not, therefore, *originate* the general liberty. It was not, at first, in his plan. The praise which belongs to him is, that he loved liberty, and that, when he felt the time had come, his natural instinct prevailed, and he put it into a decree. It was God's work; God's only; and to God be the praise. He was God's chosen instrument, sustained by that moral sense of the people, which, under the labor of the faithful men of old, came to prevail. He was the Moses, to lead God's people through the sea, and out of bondage.

With such limitations, he did the work. He found this government a slave power; he left it free. Millions of shackles were dropped.

What a glorious memory is his! The slaves called him "father." O, there will be weeping, in many a hut, in the cotton field and the rice plantation, in the sugar groves and the corn lands, when the tidings of this dastardly act of the slave power shall reach them. O, there will be mourning, in the sea-islands, at Beaufort, at Roanoke; and in Lee's old home they will wail and cry; for their friend, their father, their Moses, their prophet, is gone.

There will be rejoicing! In the heart of the arch rebel and his traitorous crew; among the slave drivers and the slave sellers; among the makers of coffles, and the forgers of fetters, and the traders in whips.

O, there will be mourning! Among the down trodden of every land, the poor, and the oppressed; among the lovers of enlightened liberty, and the haters of tyranny.

There will be rejoicing! Among the despots and the tyrants; the oppressors and their sycophants; the robbers and plunderers of men; the hypocrites who will offer pretended sympathy, with deceit in their heart.

The angels will look sadly on; and there will be jubilee in hell.

So long as history remains, so long will the name of Lincoln go down to posterity linked with the greatest act of justice the world has ever seen.

He is the illustrious martyr for liberty; the crowning sacrifice. It was slavery's blind rage that made him the victim. It was the expiring effort of that system of tyranny, which gathered together all its remaining strength, to strike down, in one last effort of revenge, the head of the nation. Sic semper tyrannis? *He* a tyrant? That he loved liberty and law was his only crime. He was only too mild, too merciful.

" Thou shalt view the land before thee; but thou shalt not go in thither."

He had come to his Pisgah. You can see him standing

upon his mount of vision, and looking into the promised land. He feels that the burden which has weighed on him for four years, is rolling off. The sacrifices of his country are nearly finished. The privations of the faithful armies are nearly at an end, and the soldier shall return to wife and child, and peaceful pursuits. The artisans of guns and swords shall make ploughshares and reapers for fruitful fields. Commerce shall flourish in now shut-up ports. A healed and powerful country shall be governed mildly. A generous nation shall show its greatness, and forgive. Amnesty shall bury the past, and we shall be brethren. Liberty shall everywhere prevail, and peace shall rule.

This was his promised land. But thou shalt not go in thither. Others shall, but thou shalt be buried on this mount. Sitting by your wife's side, in no thought of danger, without a moment's warning, — the assassin shall find you. On the day when the ruined ramparts of Sumpter receive the old flag, emblem of universal sovereignty, there is death.

It was a sad, an irreparable loss to our country. He, whose experience was so important, and in whose hands were gathered all the lines of public policy, who had won the respect of every power, and the love of his own people, who was trusted as no other man can be, — is gone. Hang listlessly, banners over us. Droop, stars and stripes. Wear black, churches and homes. For the true-hearted, God-fearing leader is gone.

But the vision is yet to be realized. The promised land is to be enjoyed. God lives. I see before us, the country united; not with the sufferance of traitors,—for they, the Canaanites are to be driven with fire and sword. I see the millions of freedmen becoming American citizens, happy and loyal. I see a land of growing wealth, in towns and cities and harvest lands. I see the ocean whitened with sails, and the harbors forests of masts. I see a flag beloved at home, and honored abroad. I see this country the asylum of the oppressed from every land. I see the name of the great republic feared by despots as no name has been since Oliver Cromwell threatened they should hear the thunder of his cannon at the gates of Rome. I see religion flourish; churches multiplied; the tread of him who preacheth glad tidings; God's Spirit descending; and the nation, tried and purified by suffering, the people of God. This day, which many Christians hail as the day when Christ arose, is the auspicious omen of this country's resurrection.

We would *he* could have seen it. It seems due to his faithfulness. But God's will be done. A nation's tears fall to the memory of a beloved ruler. A nation's heart throbs painfully at his grave. A nation's gratitude cherishes the widow and the fatherless. And in that history which will do him justice, he will be inscribed, not only as an honest, a wise, a devout ruler; but, in the story of the hard trial out of which America emerged a great and just nation, his name will be linked with its record as its martyred leader in its sufferings and its glory.

III.

*Southern Chivalry, and what the Nation ought to do with it.

Because ye have said, —
   We have made a covenant with death,
    And with hell are we at agreement; ....
When the overflowing scourge shall pass through,
Then shall be ye trodden down by it.
From the time that it goeth forth, it shall take you;
For, morning by morning shall it pass over,
By day and by night. — Isaiah, xxviii; 15, 18, 19.

—

You have seen men who have trained tigers. They reclaim, they discipline, they conquer their appetite. But, by and by, the tiger gets a taste of human blood. From that moment, the master is powerless. The eyes are the eyes of a tiger. The teeth are the teeth of a tiger. The thirst is the thirst of a tiger. Beware! Trust him not! He is a tiger! He was a tiger all the time, a quiet tiger; now he has had a taste of blood.

I told you, last Thursday, of the sin of our country. I thought it well nigh expiated. I said, " happy is the nation whose chief is imbued with such a principle," as to desire to be on the Lord's side. But little did we think that the next day's night should witness a scene which should shock the world. The expiation was not complete. I had to take the nation's chosen, beloved need.

I told you that unless the nation should do justice, there would be trouble; not *this* trouble, — we did not dream of it; but either future war, or the return of rebels to power in

---

*Preached Sunday afternoon, April 16, 1865.

Southern states. I think that God felt this. I think that His providence saw that the people were forgetting justice,— both to the traitor, in the way of penalty, and to the oppressed, both black and white. *I* feared it; and I tried to interpret to you what I knew you must feel, that the nation was in great danger of forgetting to secure what it had bought by the blood of its martyrs; and, in the tide of a too lavish generosity, omitting to exterpate the sin.

Is not God talking to us to-day? Has He not let this strange event come to startle the nation out of its weakness? Does He not say there can be no parleying with sin, no hesitation to do justice? Does He not appeal to us, not to cherish cruel revenge, but to feel that it was a tiger with whom we thought to live in peace, a tiger fired with blood? Do you want its teeth again at your throat?·

This I take to be the providential lesson of the day. And believing it to be such, as a christian minister, and as one, too, who has seen treason in the time of battle, in the throngs of wounded, and in the burial of the dead, as such do I treat it. And what I wish to show you, is What Southern chivalry is, and what the Nation ought to do with it.

It was long the feeling that a Southern Gentleman was the perfection of humanity. He was a noble, generous man, above mean and petty acts. He was no Yankee, to love a dollar. A kind of patriarchal protector, in his lordly mansion, to the attached and happy servants who could not take care of themselves. Rather passionate, but that was the natural fault of high toned feeling. His honor was proverbial. His hospitality was boundless. In government, he took the offices, — not for money, but because he was educated to statesmanship. At northern watering places, of a summer, he was feted and petted, — the generous, chivalric, Southerner. He had a right to look down on "northern mudsills" and "greasy mechanics."

It took time to find out that this was a delusion. That he was, with exceptions of course, revengeful, treacherous, murderous. That he was a liar and a cheat. That he loved money dearly, and wrung it out of the tears of his bondmen. That his lordly mansion was, nine times in ten, unfit for a sty for northern pigs. That his slaves were chained, and whipped, and branded. That his statesmanship was mere craft, to get salaries on the one hand, and, on the other to enable him to get and keep more negroes. That he was lazy, and selfish, and often stupidly ignorant. That his hospitality always wanted pay for the wayfarer's dinner, except when his ruling principle, vanity, prevented.

It took time to learn this. It did, me. I had known some honorable Southerners, so far as a slave holder can be honorable ; and I thought they were samples. But I saw the reality, in Southern lands.

But we had not really felt all this, even after this war, plotted by perjurers and felons, and carried on by barbarians. And so, to impress it upon our minds, we have had this last, this crowning evidence, of what Southern Chivalry is. It is to assassinate an unarmed man. It is to enter the room of a sick man on lying pretences, and while he lies helpless in his bed, plunge a dagger into his throat.

It was not warfare. Allowing that these people had the right to make war, — *this* was not war. To kill in fight is lawful; to assassinate is murder. An enemy, unresisting, is sacred. War, hard as it is, does not justify *every* means of injury. A soldier is an honorable man.

Nor does war justify mere revenge. When defeat comes, it cannot be repaid by useless vengeance ; it is to be accepted. A deed which would not add a single arm to the rebel force, nor weaken the hand of a single loyal soldier, which was only the work of hate and spite after remediless defeat, is not war. It is barbarism.

Nor, if revenge was ever to be palliated, could it be in this case. It was wreaked on a good, true, man; his only fault that he was observing the oath he had taken. He had never been harsh or vindictive. That very evening he had "spoken kindly of Lee and his army." He had just decided to forgive Virginia. He was planning a wide amnesty. He would not inflict lawful punishment. Then he was murdered.

But it matters not what manner of man he was. The act was the crime, on whomsoever perpetrated. That act shows us Southern Chivalry.

I. Southern Chivalry contains the elements which ensure just such deeds as this. I say " Chivalry" and not "slavery," because " Chivalry" is the sentiment back of slavery. The Slavery is an incident; the Chivalry is the principle. The Slavery does not create, it fosters only, the spirit of the Chivalry. The Chivalry merely finds Slavery one method of showing itself. Slavery is only the evidence of the rottenness of the Southern spirit.

To rob is the first characteristic of the Chivalry. The Southern Gentleman lives by robbing. His property, when he is a slave-master, is a robbery in itself. He makes men work without adequate wages. He accumulates out of toil he has stolen.

To rule without law is another characteristic. His own passions are, virtually, his only control. Laws themselves vicious, seldom enforced when good in any feature, are no restraint. He grows up a tyrant. " Every master of slaves," said George Mason of Virginia, "is born a petty tyrant." He does not, as years go on, belie the old truth that "the child is father to the man." Hence, with unrestrained passions, licentiousness is inevitable. One has only to glance at the color of the depressed race, to see the evidence. Oppression is inevitable, too. Blows and cruel punishments are at his option. He is answerable to nobody.

To kill without law, is another prerogative; or rather, it is according to law, to kill lawlessly. With "moderate chastisement" he could ensure death, and be himself harmless.

With such rights and such elements of character, it is no wonder that the slave-master should carry the disposition he has shown into general life. Moral principle was eaten out. Slavery, when made legal, poisoned truth.

When men were taught that it was right to rob blacks, it was no great stretch of principle, to rob whites. Nor to violate treaty obligations, by seizing Cuba; nor to send pirates and robbers mildly called "fillibusters," to Central America.

Without law, it was not a strange thing to carry pistols and bowie-knives; assassinate in houses and streets; lynch men who happened to think differently from the Chivalry; raise mobs to violate the obligations of the Constitution in Charleston; inflict barbarous penalties ; kidnap and sell free persons.

I have seen the gashes in the flesh of a slave-girl. Her father and her mother were both children of her master. I have seen seven hundred escaped fugitives, in one regiment; whose scars and injuries, their surgeon told me, and he showed me specimens, were beyond description. You have heard of the spots where they burned people at the stake. It was all too true. You have seen the spot where sat a Senator, at his desk in the Senate House ; where there came up behind him, a Representative of chivalric South Carolina, and beat the defenceless Senator on the head, until the brain was feared for. All this was Southern Chivalry. It was only carrying into general life, the barbarities, the cruelty, the lawlessness of education.

II. Southern Chivalry has been doing such things all through this war.

It began with perjury. Nothing more totally destitute of every sentiment of honor, than the conduct of these men while plotting treason, can be found in history. Oaths of office were nothing. They who had sworn to defend the Constitution continued to hold office to the last moment, so as to use the advantages of their official position to pull down the government. Senators, Representatives, Cabinet Officers, and small officials, with oaths fresh upon their lying tongues, were conspirators. Soldiers, educated at the expense of the nation, sworn to support the government, wearing its uniform, supported by its money, violated every oath and every obligation of honor. The Lees, and Magruders, the old Twiggs, and the Beauregards, were all traitors together. It began with stealing. Stealing moneys at Washington, at New Orleans, at Savannah ; it was only the question which could steal fastest and most. Stealing vessels, where they could find the remnant. Stealing arms, handily placed by a Virginia perjurer, who showed his Chivalry by afterwards boasting of it. Stealing forts built and armed by the nation. Stealing, even, in their condescention of littleness, mail-bags and pouches. Anything that was "portable property" was acceptable. Stealing money honestly due to northern creditors for goods furnished. Stealing all they could steal.

That was how they began; Southern Chivalry.

But they were allowed belligerent rights. How have they acted in war? For war has its rules; and no decent soldier ever violates them.

In Eastern Tennessee there were multitudes of loyal people. They must be put down. So they shot and hung unoffending citizens. They led round gray haired men till they died of exposure. They seized their property and reduced them to starvation. When they could not find the men, they hung the women in front of their homes. That was Southern Chivalry.

In Northern cities are great hotels. Full of women and children. Southern leaders plot at home, and Southern emisaries come to the cities. Here is congenial employment. It is natural to the men that have raised babies for the market; and whipped and violated women; and imprisoned women for teaching children to read. Set fire to their hotels! Do it in the night! Half a dozen at once, to make the murders surer in the confusion! Hundreds will perish in the flames! That is Southern Chivalry.

In ambulances are wounded men. The battle is over. The wounded are quietly moving on the road. Southern riders come along, open the ambulances, and shoot the helpless, unresisting captives. That was done at Front Royal. It was done in the West. I don't know how many times.

Near Tallahassee, rails are pulled up. It will destroy a train. The cars are seized and burnt. I saw the smoke. There are blacks employed on the road. They are taken out one side, and shot in cold blood. That is Southern Chivalry.

There is a fort. After heroic bravery, the garrison yields to overwhelming force. Then begins the slaughter. Surrendered men are butchered. Wounded men are made to stand up, to be shot. One is fastened to a floor by nails through his clothes; another to the side of a building; and burnt to death. The wounded are in tents and huts; and the tents and huts are set on fire. Some are burned alive, and some of them escaped to tell the tale. The murder of more than three hundred unresisting men, is the count of the good day's work. That is Southern Chivalry.

Down South there are prisoners. The captured are sent there. First, they are robbed. Then, deliberately the rebel power sets itself to destroy them by degrees. They are left shelterless, or, if sheltered, in places where they can hardly breathe; and if they go to a hole called window to get air they are shot. They are starved. What live, are skeletons; and the dead, thus cruelly and purposely murdered are counted at more than fifty thousand. That is Southern Chivalry.*

Do you wonder at these things? The wonder would be if these things did not happen. For these men were trained to this kind of work, by seven generations of oppressing, — just as they trained their blood hounds to chase men.

III. Southern Chivalry killed the President.

Possibly there are some few who yet cannot believe that this murder was anything more than the frantic idea of a single man, or a few men. The Southern leaders would not do such a thing! My friends, the Southern leaders have been doing such things for four years. It is their nature and their practice. The vile rebel at the head, — was he not a perjured traitor? Was he not responsible for the murders and starvations, while the hypocrite fasted and worshipped? The respectable general at their head, — is he not a traitor, and is not that enough to tell his corruption?

But look you at the drift.

Examine the circumstances, the letters, the remarks, atten-

---

*Gen. Lee, by virtue of his military authority, had control of this business. It was in his power, and it was his duty, to have stopped the fiendish treatment of prisoners. He did not do it. Jefferson Davis, of course, knew all about it, — if he did not plan it. Both are Southern Gentlemen!

ding this crime. Do they not all point to a plot which had its centre in Richmond?*

All along the current for four years, you have seen this thing cropping out. When the President went to Washington four years ago, who does not now know that the plot to assassinate him, then laughed at, was a reality, eluded only by skill? In Alabama, they openly said that if he reached Washington, his life was not worth a week's purchase. In Georgia, a reward was offered for his death. In repeated instances, a Brutus has been demanded to rid them of this tyrant. But a few weeks since, a Richmond paper said an event would soon happen which would "startle the world." In northern states, even, among certain classes, it has been said that he would never be inaugurated. And even a northern newspaper, in 1864, distinctly uttered the hope that the knife of the assassin might take his life.

If this particular plot was, ingeniously, ignored by Southern leaders, they cannot ignore the drift and demand of Southern feeling. Nor can the South now disclaim a act to which, at the least, their constant appeals excited the assassins. They are responsible, even if, which nobody can seriously believe, the murder was not planned in Richmond, for a mixture of English blood and Southern Chivalry to execute.

Would that this spirit was all at the South! But it is not so. In northern towns, in the old Bay State, citizens are found, so mean, so traitorous, so murderous, as to cheer when they heard that the President was assassinated! Where was the spirit of the outraged patriots of such a town, when they did not say that upon our soil such miscreants shall not live?

I have not spoken, now, of the fact that these men had no right to make war; but only of their violation of all the laws of war. Allow them belligerent rights, and their conduct is still infamous and barbarous. But I beg you to remember that they had no right to make war at all. Every act of the war was a crime.

---

*When this was said, the circumstances subsequently discovered, which would have put this position beyond question, were, of course, unknown.

The rebellion was wholly wrong. It had not an atom of apology. The Constitution was the Supreme law of the land. It was binding, and has been all these years, upon the whole country, and upon every man in it. If there had been any infraction of justice on the part of administration, there was a peaceable way of deciding it, by a court itself in the interest of the South; and there was a Senate in which the Southern interest was still dominant. But there was no infraction. It was under Buchanan's administration, and the only infraction was in the scoundrelly tyranny which found that illustrious tool a ready instrument. A constitutional election of a man pledged by himself and his party to non-interference with the legal claims of slaveholding wickedness, was no injustice. Only Southern pride was offended because it could no longer make free men beasts of burden. The war was unprovoked, and simply a crime.

The setting up of a pretended government was a crime. It had not a shadow of right. It gave to its projectors no more legal authority than they had as individuals. It could authorize them to do no act which its movers had not a lawful right to do without it; that is, its authority was wholly imaginary. It justified none of them in anything done against the constitutional authority.

Hence, every act done under this treason against the government, or against citizens, was a crime. There was no law to authorize any such act. Every man, doing such an act, was a criminal. For instance, government has the right to take property, under certain restrictions. But citizens have not. A citizen who takes it, is a robber, and his act is robbery. Hence, when the rebels confiscated property, they were merely robbers.

Government has a right to destroy, in case of disturbance. But citizens have not. Hence, when the rebels burned Chambersburg, they were guily of arson.

Government has the right to take life, for crime or in war. But citizens have not. Hence, when the rebels have killed one of our soldiers, they were murderers, and their act was murder. Every battle has been on their part, wholesale murder; nothing else, because they had no authority to take life.

All this depends on the simple principle that their pretended government was illegal, wrong, and without the shadow of authority. The fact that their act was under the color of a pretended law, does not help the matter; their pretended law was a crime.

Now add to this, that their crime was embodied in treason, was made possible by perjury, and was begun in stealing, — all to establish the infamous sin of human slavery, — and you have the Southern Gentleman. The four years of war are four years of robbery and murder by the Southern Gentleman. All to establish the rights of the Southern Gentleman, which were to breed babies for a market, trade in helpless victims of lust, whip and maim human bodies, and starve human souls.

It was, therefore, only the trained spirit of Southern Chivalry to add brutalities forbidden by the laws of war, When they sent their paroled men from Vicksburg directly into other armies, what should they care for the honor of their word, if they could defeat us at Chicamauga? A few lies more or less were of no consequence. When they shot Union soldiers after a surrender, what did they care, if it might wreak vengeance? A few murders more or less were of no consequence. What were rules of honorable warfare to men who plotted treason in the Senate chamber?

Truly the text which I have chosen is appropriate. They have made a covenant with death, and with hell are they at agreement. Their customs, their laws, their practices, were all of hell. Over that Southen land the genius of hell has long brooded. It was written in two hundred years of wronged men ground down by the slave master. It was in the cries of the scarred and the crippled. It was in the gory backs of men and women. It was in the blinded souls of their victims. It was in the ashes of the funeral stake.

Then it passed into treason, and murder.

Then it added to the crimes their treason engendered, butchered prisoners; slain women; fires at night.

Now it has shown itself in a cold-blooded, deliberate assassination of the President.

In all their course, it has, most of all, exhibited itself in its blasphemous appeals to Almighty God to defend and bless their cause!

But equally applicable is the second part of this text "When the overflowing scourge shall pass through, then shall ye be trodden down by it. From the time that it goeth forth, it shall take you. For, morning by morning shall it pass over; By day and by night."

That is God's vengeance. Faithful and true is He that promised. The cries and tears of the millions have been heard by God. They waited. They cried "is there a God?" Generations passed on; but vengeance came at last. The oppressors were crazy. In their pride they rebelled. They were their own executioners. Their stupendous crime could be reached only by their stupendous folly. "If the north fights," said Davis in 1861, "they shall smell Southern powder and feel Southern steel." Ah, they made good the boast. The wrath of God let them pile up their guilt. All the blood shed in this war lies at their door. Fearfully has it been repaid. The Southern woman dresses in black. The sons of the South lie on every battle field. Its pride — though not its venom—is quenched in blood. Their wealth is destroyed. Their towns are garrisoned by the once despised African, and negro sentinels halt the haughty Southron in Charleston and Savannah.

But it is not enough. We would, foolishly, have spared them, but they would not. It took this last blow to show the tiger, and arouse the overflowing scourge.

This blow has said to the nation,—Have you forgotten the old crimes? Have you forgotten the Senate chamber? Have you forgotten then the graves of your slaughtered sons? Have you forgotten Tennesee, and Pillow, and Andersonville? Have you forgotten Justice? Did you think kindness would tame them? Have you wanted no security?

Come, then. Stand by this bedside. Here is a sick man.

He has done his country faithful service. This is his house. Hark! there is one at the door. He *will* come in. There is a lie in his mouth. He comes to the bedside. He stabs the sick man, in the neck.

Come, again. Here is your President. His wife is with him. He has just let a rebel army go home, whose leaders ought to have been hung. He is going to pardon. See; there steals in an assassin. He shoots. The ball enters the head. The noble, faithful man is dead.

Southern Chivalry did it. Did you want this last lesson to tell you what Southern Chivalry is?

What else does it tell you?

It tells you, you have always been too lenient. You were too kind. You have played at war. Barbarians respect only force. You have not treated them rightly. In the very begining, when Baltimore fired on our troops, you should have made a street a mile wide through Baltimore. When they hung men in Tennessee, you should have hung men in Louisiana. When they shot McCook, you should have shot Buckner. When they burnt Chambersburg, you should have burned Huntsville. When they shot black prisoners at Pillow, you should have shot white prisoners in South Carolina. That is hard? It is war. War is not play; it is not for women; it is not a lullaby for your children.

It tells you to be the instrument in God's hand of cleansing the land of its pollution. You were willing to leave the freedman without a voice, to the cruelty of the old rebels, were you? You were going to leave the property and life of loyal white men to the disposal of the arch traitors, were you? You were going to let those men come back to Congress, and you would take, in yours, the hand red with your brother's blood, would you? The voice of Providence says, you must have no fellowship with iniquity.

It tells you, you must secure the country. There is but one way, — let the boys and the ignorantly deluded go; they will learn better by and by; but for the leaders, Justice!

There are practical things to do.

1. When armies fall into our hands, it should be by unconditional surrender. There should be no terms given which give to the leaders the rights of prisoners. It is a false sentiment which thinks these generals are not criminals. They are traitors, every one of them. They are murderers all. The prison should be their temporary home. The court should sit, and the judge preside; the witnesses should appear, and tell the tale; and the halter should say that treason is a crime. Rebel judges should be judged, too. Rebel statesmen should reap the reward of their plots. Without this, you are parleying with treason. You are conniving at crime.

They threaten guerrilla war. Their disbanded soldiers will rob and murder. Then let a short shrift and a sure cord be their instant fate.

2. Let the land be cleansed of persistent, sullen, rebels and households. Say to Southern Chivalry, Go; for this, our lines are open. Carry your perjuries to other shores; England is a good place for you. This land is sick of your presence. You are a stench in the nostrils of honest men. Go, Virginian discendants of transported convicts. Go, you who have lived by oppression and robbery. Never return. Your heritage is gone. Return, and the rope awaits your first step upon our shores.

3. The lands of convicted rebels should be taken. Their strength was in their possessions. Break up their estates. There are Union men by scores of thousands, who have been robbed of their all. Repay them from Southern property. There are millions of unpaid laborers at the South. Give them their arrears of wages. Place them in the lands of their birth, as owners. There are soldiers who deserve well of their country. Give them, each, a tract of land. Endow each with the musket he has faithfully borne, and tell the colonies to hold their possessions as they have held their honor and their loyalty. The men that have caused this war, — leave them landless and penniless, to do what they have

despised us for doing,— earn an honest living by the sweat of the face.

4. Let the bondmen have their rights. I told you of this last Thursday. I tell you again. It has been weighing on my mind these many days. Make these loyal men voters. It is indispensable to our security. If there are any loyal whites in the Gulf states, they ought to be glad of such reinforcements of votes as will forever secure their own safety. If there are no loyal whites there, then the blacks are all you can re-organize States with. Justice demands it, also. These men are our friends. They have been true to the government, and they ought to be trusted. They are men, and they are entitled to the rights of citizens. Put the power in their hands. Make them governors, judges, generals. Have you any doubt whether, with arms and ballots in their hands, they could hold the land? The blood which held Hayti against the power of the first Napoleon can now hold the Carolinas against whipped Southerners. The men of Wagner and Olustee are the ones to place in charge of Sumpter, and Mobile, and St. Philip.

5. Christianize that land. They need missionaries. The masses have been deceived by a corrupted Gospel. New churches are wanted there, which will acknowledge God. They need teachers, too, and schools, and civilizing processes. There is no reason to doubt the capacity of the *poor* whites to be elevated to the scale of humanity. They have good elements; they are brave, true to their convictions, and patient. *They* are not the Chivalry. You can make something of them, if you begin right and persevere.

Such things should we look to. Government will answer the wish of the people. God's providences are strange. They killed the President; but they failed to kill the one who succeeds; a man trained in Tennessee, and in all the horrors of its warfare; a man from the people, not of the Chivalry; a man who believes in reimbursing the losses of loyal men out of the property of the disloyal; a man who advocates Justice; a man who said to his black fellow citizens, when they demanded it, that he would be their Moses.

We will rally around this man. He, when generals said Nashville could not be held, sent the citizens into the trenches, and held it, and kept the flag flying. He will defend the flag as well now, and will man the ramparts with faithful men. The kindly heart is gone; the avenger has come.

By the graves of our dead comrades, by the scarred battle-flags, by the sturdy muskets, by the ashes of dwellings, let us swear eternal hatred to Southern Chivalry. In the fear of God Almighty, let us never pander to treason. Let no rebel generals be feted on our soil. Let the land be cleansed. Let the sword and the scaffold do their righteous work. Let treason die, that the country may live. By prayer, and vote, and our right arm, let us say, treason must perish. And, that treason may never have a resurrection, let Southern Chivalry be destroyed, root and branch, twig and leaf.

In the memories of this day, and because men who have violated every law, human and divine, are the enemies of God, I dare, as a Christian minister, to quote the words of the Almighty:

Arise, O God; let Thine enemies be scattered.
Pour out their blood by the force of the sword.
Let their children be scattered;
Let their wives be widows;
Let their men be put to death;
Let their young men be put to the sword.
Deal with them, in the time of Thine anger.
Wickedness is in their dwelling;
Give them according to the wickedness of their endeavors.
Give them according to the work of their hands.
Let them be as chaff before the wind.
Let their way be dark and slippery.
Let death seize upon them.

4

www.ingramcontent.com/pod-product-compliance
Lightning Source LLC
Chambersburg PA
CBHW032134080426
42733CB00008B/1074